BREAD AND ROLLS

DR ANSHUMALI PANDEY

Made with ♥ on the Notion Press Platform
www.notionpress.com

Contents

Contents

Preface

In my previous book "**Bakery Ingredients and Tools**" you have learned about the basic ingredients and their role in baking, now in this book "**Bread and Rolls**" we will be learning about making various types of bread and bread rolls. We will be learning about the various methods of making bread and various types of bread like White Pan Bread; Pullman, Split-top, and Round Split Breads; French and Italian Breads and Rolls; Vienna Bread; Bolillos; Pan de Agua; Egg Bread and Rolls; Hard Roll Varieties; Soft Roll Varieties; Pan de Sal; Rye Bread Varieties; Cornmeal Bread; Whole Wheat Bread; Raisin Bread; Cheese Bread; Indigenous Breads of India; and Middle Eastern Pita Bread.

The language used in this book is simple without any pictorial illustration to keep the cost low and affordable to all. This book is a complete handbook for anybody to even start a small bakery. This book will help students by giving them information in simple story telling style. The Author of the book is a practicing professional from the fields of Hospitality and Tourism and has an experience of over 26 years.

Happy Baking!!

Dr Anshumali Pandey

Prologue

In my previous book "**Bakery Ingredients and Tools**" you have learned about the basic ingredients and their role in baking, now in this book "**Bread and Rolls**" we will be learning about making various types of bread and bread rolls.

CHAPTER ONE

The Ideal Bread

> *"The ideal loaf should be so completely baked that when pressed upon it will immediately spring back upon release of pressure. The color should be golden brown on top sides and bottom. The loaf should be evenly raised in the pan with no cracked, uneven or protruding crusts. The bread should not taste acid or sour and the flavor should be rich and nutty. The flavor will vary with the constituents in the bread. The bread inside should have a soft velvety texture. It should not crumble when sliced. The holes should be numerous, small and uniform in size. Large holes in bread is a serious fault. The color of the bread should be slightly creamy."*

Bread is no doubt the most essential food of man. It takes the most important part in the nutrition of all classes of people. Bread is not so highly valued because of the ease of preparation but because of its nutriment, palatability, and digestibility: In it are all the substances necessary for the nutrition of man, namely; carbohydrates, proteids, fats, and mineral salts. The carbohydrates and proteids are present in about the right proportion, but the fats are deficient.

Bread is one of the most constant sources of nitrogen in the daily diet. The gluten of the flour furnishes the greater part of the nitrogen. The proportion of fat can easily be raised by the use of butter.

Another reason bread is so universally used is because of its cheapness. Considering the materials used it is cheap compared to other foods because it supplies all the necessary elements and does not require the addition of other foods to make a nourishing diet. Properly made bread is palatable by itself, and is made more so by the addition of butter, or when eaten with other foods. Bread making is by no means a modern art, it was known some 3000 B.C. Probably the first grain cultivated for use in bread - making was barley. Next came the use of wheat, which was cultivated in Egypt 4000 B.C. and in China 3000 B.C. The hone of the barley plant is in Asia Minor, that of the wheat plant in Central Asia.

The use of wheat in bread making is more universal than barley, especially in the more advanced nations. It could be truthfully said that through the cultivation of these grains civilization has been fostered. The aborigines were nomadic because they were forced to change their habitations as the source of food became exhausted. When they learned to cultivate these grains which could be stored they could remain in one place, and thus gain advantages over those who had remained nomadic.

Because of this the discovery of the use of the cereals in bread making has been described by the ancients as a gift of sod. We find many references to bread - both leavened and unleavened, in the scriptures and elsewhere. In the Lord's Prayer we ask for our daily bread. Bread is often spoken of as the "Staff of Life," and "Bread of Life." We can safely conclude that bread is a very important factor in the lives of nearly all the world's people. One of the most important factors in bread making is the leavening agent, which in nearly all cases is yeast of some sort. Since yeast is such an important factor it will be well to consider it first. Yeast was discovered by a Dutch micro-scopist about two centuries ago. The phenomenon called fermentation had been known for some 3000 years but its cause remained a mystery until the nineteenth century, when it was discovered that yeasts are the natural agents which produce fermentation.

> "*Yeast is a microscopic uni-cellular plant, belonging to the family of Fungi. The plants belonging to this'family are without chlorophyll and reproduce by buds and spores. Yeast cells have a uniform smooth outline. On the inside may be seen one or more rounded clear spots. As far as is known these are minute drops of oil, and have nothing in particular to do with the life of the cell. These drops are called vacuoles. The large dark spot is the neucleus; which appears to be floating in a semifluid which is the protoplasm of the cell. Yeast exists in three states; the resting; the growing; and he spore -bearing state.*"

The resting state is that period when the yeast cell is live but dormant, such as we find it in the dry yeast. When resting east is placed in a solution which contains proper food it begins to consume the food and grow. As it grows it multiplies by a method known as budding. Each bud appears as a little swelling on the side of the yeast cell. The bud grows until it may be as large as the mother cell, and if the plant is vigorous a second or even a third bud may have appeared. The neucleus and the other cell contents o f the mother cell divide and enter this bud, making it a complete cell. These cells may remain attached for some time and form irregular groups. When they separate they may go into the resting state or continue to develop. This depends upon the existing conditions.

This method of growth is distinctly characteristic of yeasts and separates them sharply from bacteria. Under certain conditions such as dryness and lack of food, yeast plants produce reproductive bodies known as spores. These spores are formed by the cell contents breaking up into several parts, and these parts are capable of resisting for a long time, adverse conditions, such as great heat or cold, dryness, and lack of food. Not all yeasts are known to produce spores and are sometimes classified on this basis:- those producing spores are classified as genus Saccharomyses; those not producing spores as genus Tarula. This is' Conn's classification. Jago classes all yeast fungi under the genus Saccharomyces because they mostly live in sugar solutions.

Like all members of the fungi group yeast must have warmth, oisture, air, food, and darkness in order to grow well. Between 25°C. and 35° C. yeast grows well, above or below his point the growth is not so vigorous or may be retarded altogether. Moisture is absolutely necessary to the growth of the cell. he cells must have a certain amount of water in their contents before they can grow. A sugar solution over 35% prevents the growth of the cell because the sugar has such a great affinity for water that it deprives the cell of its natural amount.

Yeast requires the presence of oxygen for its growth. Pasteur and Brown have both worked upon this particular phase of yeast life - and Pasteur states that yeast grows much better in shallow than in deep dishes - the shallow dish allowing the air to reach all the plants. Brown found that fermentation is much more vigorous in the presence of "Yeast cells can use oxygen and probably require it for Perhaps the most oxygen than in its absence. Also that: - in the manner of ordinary aerobic fungi the full completion of their life history." important condition necessary to the growth of yeast is its food. To bread makers who expect to make their own yeast, this is a very important part and should be thoroughly understood. The food materials required for yeast are sugar, nitrogenous material, and mineral matter. Of these the saccharine matter occupies the first place. This saccharine matter does not need to be in the form of sugar to begin with.

Yeast has the power to convert starchy materials into sugar. Maltose and glucoses or sugars of the C6111206 group are the only sugars capable of direct fermentation. Certain other sugars are capable of indirect fermentation by yeast. Among these are cane sugars, which however have to be first hydrolyzed to glucose by the action of the invertase or soluble diastatic body secreted by the yeast cells. Sugar of milk is incapable of fermentation by yeast. Yeast alone is unable to ferment starch paste or dextrin, these require some more powerful diastatic agent, such as malt extract.

Yeast makes use of the starchy materials indirectly through the proteids in the starchy materials. The product of this action upon the proteids converts starch paste into dextrin and maltose, which are fermentable by yeast itself. Yeast is able to secure some of its nitrogenous food material from the ammonical salts, but organic nitrogenous compounds form a more suitable nutriment. The nitrogenous material of the cell itself is utilized by the ctill; among these the soluble proteids are most apt to be used.

Pepsin forms a good yeast food. Albumin, whether egg albumin or vegetable albumin cannot be used by the cell. Pasteur has shown that when yeast is added to a solution of pure sugar and ammonium tartrate the development of cells and fermentation does not take place, but that on the addition of yeast ash, both growth of cells and fermentation occurs.

Yeast ash consists of potassium phosphate, and small quantities of magnesium and calcium phosphate. Potassium phosphate must be present, and cannot be replaced by sodium or calcium phosphates. Magnesia in the form of sulphate or phosphate is of great value to the growth of yeast. Calcium does not seem to be altogether necessary to the growth of yeast. Large quantities of mineral salts affect the shape of the yeast cell. Calcium sulphate causes the cells to be oval in outline. It is generally agreed that salt has a retarding influence upon fermentation, although quantities of salt under three per cent of the water used stimulates the growth of yeast. Jago concludes that salt from 1.4 % upwards retards alcoholic fermentation and diminishes the speed of gas evolution. It is used because it acts more powerfully as a retarding agent upon lactic and other foreign ferments. It also checks diastatic action and does not let the breaking down of the flour go too far.

Although sugar in some form is absolutely necessary to the growth of yeast, it is detrimental in too large quantities. It has such an affinity for water that solutions containing over 30 % sugar will take up the water from the yeast cells. When used in large amounts it has the effect of a preservative, and checks the growth.

The temperature most favourable to the growth of yeast is from 25° C. to 35° C. Between these points yeast grows well. Below 25° C. growth proceeds but not rapidly. At 9°

C. all action is stopped, but the cells are still alive. Freezing does not kill the cells unless they are mechanically ruptured or injured. Above 35° C. the action of yeast is weakened and at about 60° C. the proteid begins to coagulate and the yeast is destroyed. This applies only to yeast that has been moistened. Dry yeast has been heated to 100°C. without destroying it. The last condition necessary to yeast's growth is darkness. Since yeast belongs to a family lacking in chlorophyll or green coloring, light or sunlight would be injurious to its growth. The effect of light upon yeast is the same as that upon other fungi; too much light destroys its vitality. The chemical effect of yeast that interest the bread -maker is the breaking up of the sugar into alcohol and CO2.

"***The equation is as follows:-***"

"*C6H1206 = 2C2H5OH + 2 CO2*
{i.e. (Sugar)= (Alcohol)+ (carbon dioxide)}"

This production of alcohol and carbon dioxide is the foundation of all fermentations. The CO2 escapes from the surface of the yeast mixture in bubbles. One of the conditions necessary to good bread is good flour. It is hard for the inexperienced eye to detect good or bad flour by its appearance. The color is about as good an index as anything. The flour should be creamy in color. If it is very white it probably has been bleached too much,; if too yellow or gray too much of the gluten has been left in. One test used by millers and i bakers is to press a small amount into a cake then, wetting it and allowing to dry. The true color is shown much better in this way, and one cake can be used as a standard.

So much depends upon the constituents of flour in bread - making, that it should be better known in what proportions the different parts exist. The gluten which contains the proteids of the flour forms about 1/7 its weight. The main proteids in the gluten are gliadin and gluteniu: About 4.25 % of the gluten is gliadin and the gluteniu constitutes nearly all of the remaining proteid. The consistency of dough depends to a great extent upon the ratio of the gluteniu to the gliadin and little gluteniu makes a soft sticky - dough - which is too weak to raise well. Six parts of gliadin to four parts gluteniu makes a strong flour. This proportion makes the dough tough, and elastic so that it will expand under the pressure of the gas without breaking, thus making a light loaf.

Good yeast must be used if good bread is to be made. The first consideration about yeast is its strength. By its strength we mean its gas yielding power. Since the amount of gas present in part determines the lightness of the bread, yeast of good strength will make better bread than yeast of poor strength. It is better to use a small quantity of strong yeast than a large quantity of weak yeast. The strong yeast will ferment quickly and not give the foreign ferments a chance to develop, while the weak yeast will increase the time of fermentation and may be overpowered by the foreign ferments. Upon the purity of yeast the flavor of the bread depends to a great extent. A pure growth of yeast is difficult to maintain, lactic or acetic acid bacteria are present in the air, water, etc., and find a suitable medium in the yeast food. Under the head of Good Manipulation is to be considered the cleanliness of utensils. In order to have a pure growth of yeast it would be necessary to have every utensil as well as all material used - sterile.

In the ordinary process of bread -making about the only precaution taken is to sterilize the liquid used. The mere washing of the utensils does not make them clean in the true sense . Bacteria find good lodging places in nearly all utensils used. Those that cause sour bread are quite frequently introduced in that way. The handling of the bread will vary according to the methods used. The two methods most commonly used - the sponge and the dough methods differ only in the first stage. The kneading is perhaps the most important item in the working of the bread. The bread should be kneaded until smooth and velvety. It should spring back into place after being pressed with the fingers. To reach this stage usually requires about thirty minutes or more and will probably require the addition of flour during the kneading. The temperature of the hands, while handling the bread will make considerable difference. Warm hands make the dough soft and sticky. The temperature should be kept as even as possible during the period of fermentation. An increase in temperature will make the bread raise faster but it also gives lactic and other foreign ferments a start. A sudden chill will stop fermentation almost entirely. Fermentation continues until the heat of the oven kills the organisms. The same laws govern the fermentation of both sponge and dough.

Conditions that accelerate fermentation.

Yeast.

The greater the quantity the quicker it proceeds - the strength also tends to increase the rate of fermentation. Flour. Soft flours tend to hasten fermentation; they contain nore sugar and more starch in a condition susceptable to diastasis. Their proteid matter is more likely to act as a yeast stimulant, while?. the softness of the gluten lessens a physical obstacle to rapid action Of yeast.

Potatoes, Saccharine Extracts:

These act as stimulants and tend to increase the speed of fermentation.

Water:

The principal way it acts is in virtue of the proportionate quantity used. When doughs are slack fermentation proceeds much more rapidly.

Aeration:

Flour well aerated is likely to work more rapidly especially in sponges. Well beaten sponges ferment more rapidly than those not well beaten.

Temperature:

This governs all else. With low temperatures yeast works very slowly, if at all, and with higher temperatures fermentation is accelerated.

The conditions retarding fermentation may be summed up the opposite of the accelerating agents - yeast, weak or in small quantities; hard, dry flours; stiff un-aerated dough; low temperature, and addition of salt. The good baking of bread is dependent upon three conditions; the size of the loaf; the temperature of the oven; and the time in the oven. Bread should always be baked in single pans. These pans measure 9 X 4-1A X 2-3/4 (depth). This makes about a one pound l oaf. Bread baked in single pans is surer of getting baked the entire way through. Bread baked all the way through will keep much better because the yeast plants have been killed.

When two or more loaves are baked in the same pan there is little crust and the bread dries rapidly. It is more than apt to be underdone in the centre of the loaves. Besides the loaf does not look as nice as when baked alone.

The temperature of the oven for baking should be from 400 to 500 degrees Fahrenheit. The bread should not be put in on increasing heat. Too low an oven temperature allows the bread to raise too long. Too great heat forms a crust too soon and will probably blister the bread.

The bread should remain in the oven from 45 to 60 minutes, according to the size of the loaf. As soon as the bread is taken from the oven, it should be turned out of the pans. If it is allowed to stand in the pans it will sweat. Put it on a rack, right side up, and allow to cool in the open air. It should be stored in tin boxes with tight -fitting covers.

Faults of good bread, and their causes:

Faults caused by flour may be the result of moulded wheat or flour, or it may be caused by the constituents in flour. Wheat that has moulded lacks in nutritive value because the mould plant uses part of the wheat for its food. Wheat or flour is better after storage for some time. If the gliadin and glutiniu are not present in the right proportions the flour will not make as good bread. The faults caused by yeast have already been discussed more or less. Both weak yeast and foreign bacteria produce sour bread, the yeast indirectly and the bacteria directly. These bacteria may be introduced by the yeast, by dirty utensils, and through the flour.

Uncleanness of utensils adds to the sourness of bread.

Insufficient and improper kneading often give bad results in bread. The flour must be kneaded in perfectly smooth or it will make the texture poor. On contact with the air the dough forms a hard crust. This should be softened or taken off - if it is not removed it will make hard lumps in the bread. Too high temperature during fermentation makes a small loaf with poor texture. The bread usually has a clammy feeling and does not spring back upon pressure. Too high oven temperature forms a hard crust sometimes blistered, and may make the bread coarse in texture. Too low temperature makes a heavy sour loaf.

Too long fermentation weakens the yeast and allows the foreign ferments to develop. The loaf should be baked when it has risen twice its original size. If the oven is unevenly heated the loaf will raise unevenly unless it is turned constantly. The bread should not be covered when taken from the pan. Bread stored in wooden boxes is apt to absorb moisture and become mouldy.

CHAPTER TWO

The Production Stages

The Baking Process:

The basic process of baking yeast bread starts with measuring and mixing the various ingredients to make the dough and adding yeast so that it rises. The dough is then kneaded to develop the gluten and is again allowed to rise. The kneading and rising steps may be repeated several times. Next, the dough is shaped into a loaf and baked. Baking cooks the dough, firms the loaf and forms a crust on it, and improves the flavor. Finally, the loaf of bread may be sliced before being wrapped. Commercial bakeries have machines that do the work of measuring, mixing, kneading, baking, slicing, and wrapping. Skilled bakers run the machines, and nothing is left to chance. The ingredients are weighed precisely, the temperature and humidity are closely monitored, and the individual steps of the baking process are carefully timed.

Every bakery uses a special blend of flour, produced by mixing the wheat before or after it has been milled. In most large bakeries the manufacturing process begins in bins on a high floor so that gravity can draw the flour or dough from one machine down to the next. After a final sifting, the flour is fed into a scale that automatically weighs the right amount and pours it into a mixer on the floor below. Water or another liquid is poured into form dough, and yeast and other ingredients are added. The amount of flour used to make the dough can be affected by the temperature and humidity in the bakery. In addition, the temperature of the water must be exactly correct to dissolve the yeast. The yeast will be killed if the water is even slightly overheated. On the other hand its growth will be stunted by water that is too cold.

In the next step of the manufacturing process, the dough flows into huge troughs that are taken into a fermentation room. It is left there to rise for a set amount of time, usually several hours. Next, a divider scales the dough into pieces of just the right weight for the baking pans. The rounder shapes the pieces into balls, which then move through the overhead proofer. There the dough rests for a few minutes to recover from the rough dividing and rounding processes, thus ensuring tender loaves. The balls of dough drop from the overhead proofer into a molder, which shapes them to fit the baking pans exactly. The filled pans are placed in the proof box, where the final rising takes place. The proof box has a slightly warmer and moister atmosphere than that of the fermentation room. The pans then go into an oven, where they are baked at a temperature of more than 400^0F (204^0C) for about 30 minutes. Low –pressure steam is injected into the oven to prevent the crust from forming too quickly.

Most large bakeries use reel ovens or traveling ovens. A reel oven looks like an enclosed Ferris wheel, with the pans of bread on rolling racks. In a traveling oven the pans move slowly on a conveyor belt through a long baking chamber, and the bread comes out the other end.

Some traveling ovens measure more than 100 feet (30 meters) in length, and they can bake more than 5,000 loaves of bread per hour. After the loaves have been slowly cooled, a slicer cuts them into uniform slices. Finally, a wrapping machine places moisture –proof paper around each loaf and seals the paper to keep the bread fresh and protect its flavor. The loaves are then packed into trucks and taken to stores. The process of making unleavened bread, which is sometimes called no –yeast bread or quick bread, is much simpler than that used for yeast bread. Since the dough contains no yeast, kneading and rising are not involved. The procedure consists merely of measuring and mixing the ingredients and then shaping the dough and baking it.

Bakeries make many products in addition to bread, including rolls, crackers, biscuits, and such pastries as cookies, cakes, pies, and doughnuts. Machines do much of the work in baking these products, as in making bread. Bakers use a variety of devices for molding and cutting and for such operations as making and applying frosting and icing. There are two general kinds of cakes butter cakes and sponge cakes. Butter cakes contain butter or some other fat, plus flour, sugar, eggs, leavening, milk, salt, and flavoring. Bakers make many varieties of these cakes by adding chocolate, molasses, spices, nuts, coconut, or other ingredients. Sponge cakes, such as angel food cakes and similar products, have no fat. They usually consist of flour, eggs, sugar, salt, and flavoring. The eggs provide the liquid, and the air for rising as well, and cream of tartar is added for lightness and tenderness.

STRAIGHT DOUGH METHOD:

In this method all the ingredients are mixed together, and the dough is fermented for a predetermined time. The fermentation time of straight dough depends on the strength of flour. Strong flours require more fermentation time to mature adequately. Flours which require 2 to 3 hours for maturing should be used for making bread by straight method. Flours that take very long period for maturing should not be used in straight method because during prolonged fermentation periods it is very difficult to control the temperature of dough and rise in temperature will invariably cause acid taste and flavour in bread. As temperature rise has immediate effect on fermentation speed, it is very necessary to control the temperature of straight dough by;

- Using shorter fermentation periods
- Adjusting the temperature of doughing water
- By fermenting the dough at optimum (room) temperature i.e. between 78 to 80^0F.

When it is desired to ferment straight dough for longer period, it should be remembered that gluten will soften up to a greater extent and is likely to become sticky; therefore the dough should be made tighter. Yeast content should be reduced but sugar content should be increased in order to provide food during prolonged fermentation. Salt content is increased as it provides stability to the dough and keeps the fermentation speed under control which is necessary during long fermentation period.

Salt–Delayed Method:

This is a slight variation of straight method, where all the ingredients are mixed except salt and fat. As the salt has a controlling effect on enzymatic action of yeast, the speed of fermentation of a salt less dough will be faster, and a reduction in total fermentation time could be affected. The salt is added at the knock –back stage. The method of adding salt at the later stage may be according to the convenience of individual baker. It may be sifted (dry) on the dough and mixed. It may be creamed with fat and mixed. Whatever way is chosen for mixing the salt, only three –fourth (of the actual mixing time) mixing should be given initially and one – fourth mixing at the time of adding salt. The method is especially suitable if strong flours are to be used for bread making by straight method. Due to absence of salt, the fermentation speed enhanced and gluten is matured in a reasonably shorter time.

No Time Dough Method:

In this method, dough is not fermented in a usual manner. It is just allowed a brief period (about 30 min), for it to recover from the strains of mixing. Since dough is not fermented the twin functions of fermentation (i.e. production of gas and conditioning of gluten) are achieved to some extent by increasing the quantity of yeast (2 to 3 times of original quantity) and by making the dough little slacker and warmer. Although it is possible to make fairly acceptable bread (during emergency) by using this method the product has poor keeping quality and lacks in aroma. Due to absence of fermentation the gluten and starch are not conditioned sufficiently to retain the moisture and there is no flavour because flavour producing bi –products of fermentation are absent. As there is increased quantity of yeast present, the bread may have a strong yeast flavour.

Sponge and dough method:

Previously, in this chapter it has been mentioned that strong flours take too long for conditioning and should not be used for making bread by straight dough method. For such flours sponge and dough method is more suitable where the problem of controlling the dough temperature is not so acute as the total fermentation time is divided in two separate segments. For the sake of convenience and proper identification, sponge dough is indicated at 60/40 sponge –dough, or 70/30 sponge –dough, where the first numbers i.e. 60 or 70 indicate the percentage of flour used in sponge and the second numbers i.e. 40 or 30 indicate the percentage of flour mixed at the time of dough making.

In this method, as a first step, a part of flour, proportionate amount of water, all the formula yeast and yeast food are mixed together. Longer fermenting sponges may contain some amount of salt also. Mixing operation is carried out just sufficiently to incorporate all the ingredients evenly. This sponge is fermented for predetermined time. Sponge fermentation time depends on the amount of flour in the sponge and flour quality. The quantity of flour in sponge depends on the strength of flour. If the flour is too strong, more quantity should be used in sponge and in turn the sponge should be fermented for longer duration. It is advisable to test the sponge physically for its readiness before mixing it into dough.

The following methods of sponge testing could be used;

Take a small piece of sponge and try to break it with both hands. If the piece breaks with a clean fracture the sponge is ready for mixing. If sponge is not ready, the piece will stretch to some extent and will break in unevenly stretched shreds. In such case sponge should be allowed more fermentation time.

Tear the sponge apart from the center with both hands and examine the web structure. If the web structure is very fine, the sponge is ready. An adequately fermented sponge feels dry to touch without any stickiness present. When the sponge is ready, it should be broken down properly with formula water, so that its even mixing in the dough is assured. Uneven mixing of sponge in the dough should be avoided as it produces uneven results in the bread. Broken down sponge is mixed with the remaining flour, sugar, salt, fat etc. Mixing operation should be carried out to the right degree. If two different kinds of flour are at hand, the weaker flour should be used at the time of dough making.

After the dough is mixed, it is rested for 30 to 45 min. during which time it relaxes from the stress of mixing operation. Pre –conditioned gluten of the sponge hastens the conditioning process of the gluten of fresh flour during this period and the dough is in perfect state for further manipulation i.e. cutting, moulding etc.

Ferment and Dough Process:

This is a variation of sponge and dough method. Very often a (bread product) formula may contain milk, eggs, substantial quantity of fat and sugar as in the case of sweetbread, Danish pastry and other sweet fermented products. All these formula ingredients will have a retarding effect on yeast activity. If all the formula yeasts, part of flour, yeast food and sufficient water (to make a fluid batter as in case of flying ferment) are mixed together, the yeast gets initially an environment which is conducive to vigorous activity and the end of fermentation time (of ferment) it is in a fit condition to take on the extra load of fermentation in the presence of milk, eggs, excessive fat etc. Fermentation time of ferment depends on the formulation of the product desired to be made and the flavor desired in the product but very often it becomes a matter of individual preference eg. some bakers may take the ferment (for mixing) after it is dropped by itself , while others may take it just prior to dropping and some may allow time even after it has been dropped. A ferment containing milk should be guarded against over fermentation as it will develop more than desirable quantity of lactic acid which in turn will affect the flavour, taste and texture of the product.

When ferment is ready, it is mixed into dough, along with the remaining ingredients and allowed to ferment for the second stage of fermentation before the dough is taken up for makeup. This method is used for making enriched bread, buns, Danish pastry, sweet dough, doughnuts etc. where the speed is very necessary.

Characteristics of a quality bread and bread roll:

Every type of bread has its own requirements and quality characteristics. The quality of bread is a function of its ingredients, yeast activity and processing conditions. The soft and resilient texture and fine cell structure (grain) of a slice of white pan or whole wheat bread, are features that consumers expect when purchasing these breads. An "ideal" or high –quality loaf of white pan bread should have the following characteristics –

Internal:

- ***Grain***– small (tight) cells, very thin cell walls, fine and uniform cell size distribution in center, elongated and fine cells around perimeter.
- ***Crumb color***– bright white or slightly creamy.
- ***Flavor***– slightly sweet, yeasty and aromatic flavor of baker's yeast mixed in flour –and –water dough. Strong and sharp fermentation flavors are not desired.
- ***Aroma***– when bread is smelled, close to the nose, while inhaling deeply, the aromatic sensation experienced is described as bread aroma.
- ***Tactile crumb texture***– smooth and silky feel. Crumb should be resilient when pressing lightly with the fingers.
- ***Mouth feel***– moist and soft (dry or gummy mouth feel are not desired).

External:

- ***Loaf volume***– good loaf volume with optimum oven spring. Sufficient rise renders proper break and shred.
- ***Break and shred***– break and shred should be high and fairly smooth, not excessive or rough or bulging.
- ***Uniformity of shape***– symmetrical with a rounded top (flat top and irregular shapes are not desired). Loaf should retain a straight and upright position. Keyholing, collapsing, flat top and uneven shape are considered defects.
- ***Crust color***– well –developed golden –brown color, smooth and even.
- ***Crust surface***– side walls and top crust should be smooth and should not contain holes or pits.

CHAPTER THREE

Common Faults Committed while Making Bread

Flaked Crust also known as Flying Tops:

If fermented dough is left uncovered in an atmosphere which is not saturated with moisture (80-85 per cent), water evaporates from the surface of the dough leaving the skin dry. This skin, once formed, is difficult to eliminate and when a skinny dough is knocked back, scaled, and moulded; the dry skin, breaks off and some which remain on the exterior will get folded into the dough and show as whitish coloured patches which are hard and knotty. When moulded dough pieces become skinned and it will give an unsatisfactory bloom of the crust. Also there will be a number of bursts or 'flying tops'.

Lack of Volume:

Bread not fermented enough has a lack of volume. This fault can be said to be a direct effect of the insufficient ripening of the gluten. It has already been discussed in detail how fermentation affects the gluten structure and the final flavour of the bread. Over fermentation may also be a reason for lack of volume in bread. Longer fermentation time increases the acid production giving a very sour taste. This activity will weaken the gluten for lack of volume and large holes. It will also give a bad structure to the baked bread which will begin to crumble easily.

Other reasons for lack of volume are:

i. Breads not proved for required length of time;

ii. Due to improper mixing of the dough, the gluten does not develop, which is directly responsible for the volume of the bread;

iii. Too much salt in dough;

iv. Less yeast in the dough;

v. too high oven temperatures.

Uneven Texture, Showing Large Irregular Holes:

i. When the dough is not fermented long enough the gluten will not reach its maximum extensibility. As the gluten is not fully extended, the loaf will be smaller in volume. Also, some of the smaller gluten strands will break down under the expansion pressure of the gas, creating irregular large sized holes in the baked product.

ii. Use of over fermented dough.

iii. Under proved bread may show a crack on the base, thereby giving an irregular shape to the bread.

Lack of Shine on the Crust:

i. Under fermented bread. The sheen of the crumb depends upon the structure of the gluten formation, as kneading increases number of fine glossy cell surfaces to reflect the light. Greater the web like structure of the gluten greater will be the reflection of the light.

ii. Use of over fermented dough.

Lack of Flavour and Aroma:

i. Use of under fermented bread.

ii. Use of over fermented dough, which also gives a slightly acidic flavour to the bread.

Stales Rapidly:

i. Bread not fermented for required time.

ii. Not enough salt used in dough.

iii. Over proved bread.

Crumbly Bread:

i. Use of over fermented dough.

ii. Use of over proofed dough.

iii. Not enough fat used in dough.

Lack of Colour on Crust:

i. Use of over fermented dough.

ii. Insufficient sugar in the dough.

Raw Inside:

i. Under baking of the bread.

ii. Baking done in high temperature, whereby the crust has got a colour but is doughy in the center.

Rope:

Rope is one of the main diseases that affect the bread. The spores of bacillus mesentericus vulgatus, the microorganisms, is responsible the development of the rope. It is usually present in the flour itself. This is not apparent until the bread is some hours old. This develops in the form of patchiness and the crumb becomes sticky. At the same time a peculiar odour similar to that of pineapple develops. This will occur only when the spore is given suitable conditions for it to develop, increase, grow, and so produce an attack of the disease. These conditions include warmth, moistness, and a deficiency of acid in the medium. Spores cannot develop in an acid medium. Also as the spores require warm weather rather than the cold, it becomes even more important to cool the bread quickly and completely. This can prevent by the using sour dough in the making of the bread, as sour dough will have a sufficient acid content to prevent the formation of rope. This is also called the 'mature parent dough' method.

CHAPTER FOUR

WHITE PAN BREAD

White bread typically refers to breads made from wheat flour from which the bran and the germ layers have been removed (and set aside) from the whole wheat seed as part of the flour grinding or milling process, producing a light colored flour. This milling process can give white flour a longer shelf life by removing the natural oils from the whole grain. Removing the oil allows products made with the flour, like white bread, to be stored for longer periods of time avoiding potential rancidity. In the United States, consumers sometimes refer to white bread as sandwich bread and sandwich loaf.

Recipe

Ingredients –

- Instant yeast – 4 . tsp
- Warm water(divided) – .cup+ 2⅔ cups
- Granulated sugar – .cup
- Salt – 1 tbsp
- Unsalted butter 3 tbsp
- All –purpose white flour 9 to 10cups
- Unsalted butter(melted, for brushing) – 3tbsps

Method –

- In the bowl of a mixer, stir to dissolve the yeast in a cup of the warm water, and let sit for 5 minutes.
- Add the remaining water, sugar, salt, room temperature butter, and 5 cups of the flour and stir to combine.
- Using a dough hook, mix on low speed and gradually add the remaining flour until the dough is soft and tacky, but not sticky (you may not need to use all of the flour).
- Continue to knead until a soft ball of dough forms and clears the sides of the bowl, about 7 to 10 minutes.
- Place the dough in a lightly greased bowl and turn it over so it is completely coated. Cover with plastic wrap and set in a draft –free place to rise until doubled in size, about 45 minutes to 1 hour.
- Turn the dough out onto a clean, lightly floured surface. Gently press it all over to remove any air pockets.
- Divide the dough in two and, working with one piece at a time, gently pat it into a 9x12 inch rectangle, starting from the short end into a very tight cylinder.
- Pinch the seams and the ends and tuck and place the roll into a 9 inch loaf pan.
- Cover the laves loosely and place them in a draft free area until it is double its size which take about 40 minutes.
- Position an oven rack on the lowest setting and preheat the oven to 400 degrees F.
- Brush the loaves with some of the melted butter.
- Bake the loaves for 30 to 35 minutes, rotating halfway through, until golden brown. (thermometer inserted into the center should read 195 degrees F).
- Remove from the oven and immediately brush with more of the melted butter.

- Allow to cool for 10 minutes, then remove from the pans and cool completely before slicing.
- The bread can be stored in an airtight bread bag or wrapped tightly in plastic wrap at room temperature for up to 4 days. It can also be frozen for up to 1 month.

CHAPTER FIVE

PULLMAN

A pullman pan (also known as a pain de mie pan) has a lid. Rather than having the flared sides of a typical bread pan, this one has straighter sides. The lid performs several different functions. First, it keeps the bread confined, which means it can't rise as much as it wants to. This affects the crumb structure; you won't get big bubbles.

Second, the bread comes out of the pan with a square top. It's actually pretty square all around. It makes nice sandwich bread and if you need to cut the crusts off for presentation, you won't have a lot of waste.

Third, since it cooks in that confined space, the steam from the cooking bread doesn't escape the way it does when you cook free-form, or even in an open pan.

Recipe:

Ingredients:

- 1 1/2 cups lukewarm water
- 1 cup (5 1/2 ounces) semolina flour
- 2 tablespoons honey
- 2 1/4 teaspoons instant yeast
- 2 cups (9 ounces) bread flour
- 1/2 cup white wheat flour
- 1 1/2 teaspoons salt

- 3 tablespoons butter

Method:

- In the bowl of your stand mixer, combine the water, semolina flour, honey, yeast, and bread flour. Stir to combine. Cover and set aside for 20 minutes.
- Add the white wheat flour, salt, and butter and knead with the dough hook attachment of your stand mixer until the dough is smooth and elastic. Flour your work surface lightly, and knead by hand briefly, then form the dough into a ball. Drizzle with olive oil and return it to the bowl. Cover with plastic wrap and set aside for 30 minutes.
- Preheat the oven to 350°F (175°C). Turn out the dough and knead it briefly to knock out the large bubbles. Form it into a log about 13 inches long - to fit inside the pan. Place the log in the pan, seam-side down. Put the lid on the pan and set aside until the dough has risen to within about an inch of the top of the pan - about 40 minute (but you might want to check at 30 minutes, just in case).
- Bake until the loaf is golden brown, about 40 minutes. Remove the loaf from the pan and allow it to cool completely on a rack before slicing.

CHAPTER SIX

SPLIT –TOP

SPLIT –TOP

Split –top pan bread –When the dough has been put in the loaf pan, but before it goes into the oven, a knife has been used to make a shallow cut into the top of the loaf. This cut releases the tension on the bread and lets it rise higher, giving it a lighter texture and a softer crumb. Example Bloomers and Vienna bread. Bloomer refers to a bread shape that is cylindrical, but flat on the bottom with several diagonal slashes across the top. The term most often describes a bread shape popular throughout Britain. Bloomers are made with many types of flour, although various types of wheat flour are the most popular. The Vienna shape describes an Oval loaf that is tapered at the ends.

ROUND SPLIT BREADS

These breads are round shaped breads in which cross splits in the upper side is done while panning. Cob is a term that refers to a large, rounded, top split plain loaf that can be made with various types of flour. Cob is a term that usually describes rounded loaves in Britain, while boule is a term that describes similar bread with criss-cross split in France. A Coburg is similar to a cob except that it has a cross slashed into the top. The method of preparation is similar to Vienna bread.

CHAPTER SEVEN

VIENNA BREAD

Vienna bread or pain Viennois is a type of bread that is produced from a process developed in Vienna, Austria, in the 19th century. It is normally made in the shape of a baguette, though the crust is softer than a baguette, the texture is finer, and the taste is sweeter. Viennese bakers use either brewers' yeast or a ferment, prepared by themselves, of which the basis is an infusion of hops.The loaves have horizontal slashes on top and glazed with egg wash and topped with sesame seeds or poppy seeds before baking. The ideal bread for toast and all sandwiches from hot dog to the top notch sandwich such as beer –braised pulled pork with orange barbeque sauce and coleslaw sandwich. Initially it was bread was made only from beer yeast, but nowadays brewer's yeast is used.

Recipe

Ingredients –

- Lukewarm water – 325 ml
- Active dry yeast – 14 gms
- Sugar – 2 tbsps
- Milk powder – 30 gms
- Refined white flour – 500 gms
- Salt 1 – tbsp or to taste

- Butter (unsalted) – 3 tbsps
- Egg white – for brushing (or milk)

Method –

- To begin making Pain Viennois or Vienna Bread Recipe, in a bowl, combine water, sugar, yeast and milk powder in a big mixing bowl. Allow it to stand for 10 minutes until bubbly and frothy.
- Add the flours, salt and butter to the yeast mixture and knead them to a dough.
- Later transfer it over a work surface and continue kneading until smooth and pliable for about 10 minutes. Do not use any extra flour while kneading or shaping.
- Place the dough in a greased bowl and cover the container with a plastic wrap. Set aside in a warm place until almost tripled in volume.
- Transfer the proofed dough on to a flat working surface and knead the dough for a minute or two to release the trapped air. Divide the dough into 9 equal pieces and shape them into tight round balls. Place them on a baking sheet and rest them for about 15 minutes.
- Flatten each dough ball to remove the air bubbles and shape them into tight 8 inch logs. Place 4 to 5 logs over each baking tray lined with parchment paper.
- Brush their tops with milk or beaten egg. Carefully score each log horizontally 12 to 15 times with a sharp blade or razor. Allow them proof for about an hour until doubled.
- Bake them in a preheated oven at 450 degree fahrenheit for about 15 minutes rotating the trays half way through to ensure equal baking.

- Remove the baked buns and cool them on a wire rack to room temperature. Vienna bread stays good for upto 2 days at room temperature and can be freezed for upto 3 weeks.

CHAPTER EIGHT

BOLILLOS

A bolillo or pan francés (meaning "French bread") is a type of savory or sweet bread traditionally made in Mexico, but also made in Central America. It is a variation of the baguette, but it is ovoid shaped and shorter in length and is often baked in a stone oven.It is also known as *birote* and *pan blanco* in some areas of the country.

Recipe

Ingredients –

- Warm water – 2 cups
- Active dry yeast – 1 (¼ –ounce) packet
- Bread flour – 4 cups
- Salt – 1 tsp
- Sugar – 1 tsp
- Egg white (whisked) – 1

Method –

- Pour water into a large mixing bowl, and sprinkle yeast onto the surface of the water.
- In a separate mixing bowl, mix flour, salt, and sugar.
- Add flour mixture to water a little at a time, mixing until a dough forms.

- Place dough in a greased bowl, cover with a towel or cloth and leave in a warm place for about an hour.
- Remove dough from bowl, punch it down and knead for about 10 minutes.
- Divide dough into 10 balls.
- For oval –shaped rolls (the usual bolillo shape), roll the balls between your palms for about 5 seconds to make a cylindrical shape, tapering slightly at the ends.
- Place pieces on one or more baking sheets.
- Cover and let loaves rise again for about 30 minutes.
- Preheat oven to 375^0F / 190^0 C.
- Brush each dough ball with egg white. Score each roll with two, 2 –inch lines along the top, about ¼ –inch deep.
- Bake loaves for about 30 minutes.
- Remove from oven; cool slightly and eat warm, or let cool completely and store tightly covered.

CHAPTER NINE

PAN DE AGUA

This Puerto Rican water bread **(*pan de agua*)** is similar to French, Italian bread or Cuban bread because it's made from the same basic ingredients, but the baking process is different. It is made in entire Spanish Caribbean. The dough is placed in a cold oven and is set above a pan of boiling water. The bread continues to rise as the oven heats, causing light colour crust to become deliciously thin and crisp and slightly sweeter in taste.This bread is first kept in a cold oven with a cup of hot water below it for ten minutes. Thereafter the oven is switched on and the bread is baked.The bread can be eaten as is or with butter or even used to make sandwiches.

Recipe:

Ingredients –

- Flour – 5 cups
- Salt – 1 tbsp
- Sugar – 1 tbsp
- warm water – 2 cups
- yeast (rapid rising) – 1 tbsp
- egg white – 1
- water – 1 tbsp
- cornmeal or flour – to dust the pan

Method –

- Lightly whisked together 1 egg white and 1 tbs of water, keep aside.
- Mix flour and salt together and set aside.
- In a separate bowl mix sugar, water and yeast, and let stand for 20 min (with a towel over the top of the bowl).
- Start adding your dry ingredients one cup at a time. Stir it together each time you add more.
- When about ¾ of a cup left, dust the counter with a little flour (and start kneading the dough for about 8 –10 minutes.
- Slowly add the rest of the flour mixture to the counter and/or the actual dough while you are kneading, until all the flour is used up and 10 min has passed.
- Place the kneaded dough in a very deep greased bowl. Cover it damp cloth and put to rest for 2 hours.
- When it's done, sprinkle just a bit of fresh flour on the counter and dump your dough on it. The part that was touching the bowl should be a bit sticky which means that the dough is perfect.
- Next, take a knife and cut the dough in half. Form two long loaves and place in a non –stick –sprayed baking sheet with cornmeal (or flour) sprinkled on it. Take a sharp knife, and cut slits all across the top of the loaves.
- Brush the dough with egg white and water mixture.
- Once all this is done, boil a little over a cup of water (about 1¼ cup).
- Place loaves the middle of the oven. On the bottom rack place a shallow pan with the boiling water.
- Turn your oven on 400^{0}f and bake for 35 min. Do not pre –heat your oven. Just turn it on once all it in there.

CHAPTER TEN

EGG BREAD AND ROLLS

Fluffy, soft, enriched with both eggs and butter and slightly sweeter in taste. These are great for breakfast with butter and jam or accompanying a comforting meal at dinner time. Example is Challah, which is a special bread in Jewish cuisine,

Recipe

Ingredients –

- Lukewarm water – ½ cup
- Lukewarm whole milk – 1 cup
- Instant yeast – 2 tbsp
- Sugar – 1 tsp
- Beaten egg – 1 large
- For brushing – 1 egg
- Butter – 30 gms
- All –purpose flour – 4 + ½ cups
- Salt – 3/4 tbsp

Method –

- In the bowl of a stand mixer fitted with the dough hook, stir together the water, milk, butter, sugar, and dry yeast.
- Let it stand for approximately 10 minutes, or until the yeast starts to bubble. Add in the egg and stir to combine well.
- Add in the salt and mix with the flour. Keep adding flour a bit at the time, still stirring until absorbed.
- Then, with the mixer on low speed, gradually add in the remaining flour until combined. Increase speed to medium and knead until the dough is smooth and elastic. Rest for about 10 minutes.
- Shape the dough into a ball and place inside a greased mixing bowl. Cover with plastic wrap, keep it into warm place and allow to rise until doubled in size, about 1 ½ to 2 hours.
- Punch the dough down. Now the dough is ready to be shaped and used as you wish. You can make bread, differently shaped rolls, pizza or dinner rolls with this all – purpose dough.
- This amount of dough makes 5 rolls at 90 gms each or 8 smaller ones at 56 gms, 1 pizza, 1 bread loaf.
- It usually weights just a bit over 1 pound of dough. Double the amount if you wish to make more rolls.

CHAPTER ELEVEN

HARD ROLL VARIETIES

These are made from lean yeast dough which is low in fat and sugar. Only the bare essentials – flour, yeast, salt and water – are used to make it. Its crust is hard and crumbles easily and can be kept for a long time. Spices, herbs, dried nuts, and fruit may be added, but very little (if any) sugar and fat is included. These are prepared by straight dough method and are mostly used in French and Italian cuisines.

Recipe

Ingredients –

- Sugar – 2 tbsp
- Active dry yeast – 1 tbsp
- Salt – 2 tsp
- Warm water – 1 ½ cup
- Butter (soft) – 3 tbsp
- Egg white – 1
- Bread flour – 4 ½ to 5 ½cups
- Cornflour – ¼ tsp
- Water – ½ cup
- Cornstarch – 1 tsp

Method –

- In a large bowl, mix sugar, yeast, salt, and water until yeast is dissolved. Add butter, egg white, and 3 cups of flour. Mix until well blended. Slowly add flour, about a ¼ cup at a time, until dough is formed.
- Turn dough out onto floured board and knead for 8 minutes, adding small amounts of flour to the dough as necessary.
- Place dough in greased bowl. Turn dough over in a bowl to grease dough top. Cover and let rise for 45 minutes or until double in size.
- Punch down dough. Turn out onto lightly floured board, cover dough and let sit for another 10 minutes.
- Prepare two large baking sheets by greasing the sheets and sprinkling cornflour on them.
- Divide dough into two equal parts. Divide each half into 9 equal pieces for a total of 18 rolls. Form each dough piece into round ball and place on baking sheet, leaving about 3 inches space between rolls. Cover rolls and let rise for about 30 minutes or until double in size.
- Mix water and cornflour in small saucepan. Bring to boil and then set aside to cool to warm until rolls are finished rising.
- Brush rolls with cornstarch mix and cut an X on roll tops. If desired, sprinkle rolls with sesame or poppy seeds.
- Bake rolls at 450 F for about 15 minutes or until done. Remove from baking sheets and let cool on wire racks. Let rolls cool completely before bagging and freezing for later.

CHAPTER TWELVE

SOFT ROLL VARIETIES

These are made from lean yeast dough which is fairly high in fat and sugar and have soft crust.The amounts of fat and sugar vary from 6 percent to 9 percent.They're pillow soft with the most delicious flaky and buttery texture. They are commonly called dinner rolls. They can be made more sweeter by adding extra sugar. The softer and richer the bread, the more fat in the dough. This is known as rich dough. The method of preparation is straight dough method.

Few varieties of soft rolls include –

Buns –is a small, sometimes sweet, bread –based item or roll. Though they come in many shapes and sizes, they are most commonly hand –sized or smaller, with a round top and flat bottom. They are usually made from flour, sugar, milk, yeast and butter. Common sweet varieties contain small fruit or nuts, and may topped with icing or caramel, or filled with jam or cream. Some types of buns are filled with various meats, or used to serve meats (such as hotdogs or hamburgers). They are served in every dinner in Great

Britain.

Challah –these are braided buns with 3 –6 braids. It is a Jewish specialty.Challah has a noticeably higher level of eggs than the other doughs on this list, which contributes to its especially golden crust and often yellowish interior crumb.

Monkey Bread –The origin of the term "monkey bread" comes from the pastry being a finger food; the consumer would pick apart the bread as a monkey would. This American bread recipe is made in a bundt cake pan to create a donut –shaped cake that's easy to pull apart. It is covered with butter and sugar and sometimes with vanilla ice cream. It can be taken as breakfast, brunch, or dessert.

Brioche –is classic French yeast very 'rich' bread. Whereas standard breads can be made only with water, flour, salt and yeast, a brioche will contain plenty eggs, milk and butter. The high fat and protein contents of these ingredients are what make the bread so special. Fresh brioche can be served with jelly or other preserves to accompany tea or coffee, or with pate or hors d'oeuvre.

Croissant –or crescent rolls are French buttery, flaky, *Viennoiserie* pastry of Austrian origin, named for its historical crescent shape. The yeast –leavened dough is layered with butter, rolled and folded several times in succession, then rolled into a sheet, in a technique called laminating. The process results in a layered, flaky texture, similar to a puff pastry. They are a common part of a continental breakfast in many European countries.

Cinnamon Rolls –are made up of flattened rich dough that has been spread with cinnamon and sugar, then rolled and sliced into glorious swirls of buttery pastry and gooey filling. They are served commonly in Northern Europe and North America. In Sweden it is called *kanelbulle*, in

Denmark it is known as *kanelsnegl*, in Norway it is known as *Skillingsboller*, It is commonly eaten in breakfast or coffee break or as dessert.

Sticky Buns –These are a type of dessert or breakfast sweet roll that generally consist of rolled pieces of leavened dough — sometimes containing brown sugar or cinnamon

compressed together to form a kind of flat loaf corresponding to the size of the pan in which they are to be baked. Before the dough is placed in the baking –pan, the latter is lined with the "sticky" ingredients, such as brown sugar, honey (or both), as well as nuts and raisins and perhaps more sugar and sometimes butter. After the buns are baked, they are inverted so that the pan lining then becomes a topping. They originated in Pennsylvania with German settlers.

Recipe of BUN:

Ingredients –

- Bread flour – 725 gm
- Milk/water – 400 ml
- Instant yeast – 10 gm
- Salt – 2 tsp
- Sugar – 80 gm
- Nonfat milk solids – 40 gm
- Soft butter – 40 gm
- Melted butter – 30 gm
-

Method –

- Combine ½ flour, yeast, sugar, salt, milk, butter, in the bowl of a stand mixer.
- Attach the dough hook and turn the mixer on to the lowest speed and mix until flour is incorporated, scraping down the sides of the bowl as necessary. Increase speed to medium and beat for 2 minutes.
- Add ½ flour and blend with the dough hook until incorporated. And another ½ flour and repeat, mixing at medium speed for another 2 minutes until a ball of dough is formed.
- Add additional flour as necessary. The dough should be slightly sticky and soft and pulling away from the edge of the bowl.
- Transfer the dough to a lightly greased bowl and cover with a towel or plastic wrap. Let rise for 30 minutes at room temperature.
- Remove the towel or plastic wrap and deflate the dough by punching down lightly.
- Pinch off pieces of the dough and form 24 rolls. Transfer the rolls to a lightly greased quarter baking sheet or 9 x 13 baking dish. Cover with a towel or plastic wrap and let rise for an additional 30 minutes at room temperature.
- Preheat oven to 375 degree F. Bake the rolls for 12 to 15 minutes or until golden brown and cooked through. If the rolls are getting too brown, just tent the rolls with foil.
- Remove rolls and brush hot rolls with the melted butter. Serve immediately or store cooled rolls in a plastic bag for up to 3 days.

CHAPTER THIRTEEN

PAN DE SAL

It is a type of Filipino yeast –raised bread that is slightly sweet and baked as small, oval loaves. The name comes from the Spanish pan de sal, which literally means *'bread of salt'*. Pandesal is the most popular bread in the Philippines. In the sixteenth century, it was also called *"the bread of the poor"* because it was an alternative to rice during the Philippines revolution. According to the story, pan de sal was originally to be modeled on French bread, the ancestor of French baguette, made from wheat flour, baker's yeast, sugar, water and salt. It is most commonly served hot and may be eaten as is, or dipped in coffee, hot chocolate or milk. It can also be complemented with butter, margarine, cheese, jam, peanut butter, chocolate spread, or other fillings like eggs, sardines and meat.

Recipe

Ingredients –

- All –purpose flour – 4 + ½ cups
- Active dry yeast – 2 ¼ tsp
- Warm milk – 1 ¼ cup
- Salt – 1 tsp
- Sugar – ½ cup
- Canola oil – 1/3 cup

- Eggs lightly beaten – 2 large
- Bread crumbs – dusting the pandesal dough

Method –

- Stir together the warm milk, yeast and about a tbsp of the sugar in the bowl of a stand mixer. Let this mixture stand until it is foamy. In another bowl, combine 4 cups of flour and salt.
- Once the yeast mixture is foamy, add in the eggs, sugar and oil to the bowl of stand mixer.
- Gradually add the flour mixture, about a cup at a time while stirring with a wooden spatula or spoon. Briefly mix everything together until a shaggy dough forms.
- Attach the dough hook to the stand mixer and run the mixer on medium speed to start kneading the dough.
- After ten minutes of mixing, gradually sprinkle little amounts of flour to the dough (about a tbsp at a time) to help in the kneading process.
- Continue to knead until the dough gathers in the center and is cleaning the sides and bottom of the bowl.
- This should take about 20 minutes or so and you should only have used up to ½ cup of flour.
- Gather the dough into a ball. Place it inside a bowl, cover with a kitchen towel and let stand in room temperature to rise for an hour, or until size is doubled. Meanwhile, line a large baking sheet with parchment paper.
- Gently deflate the dough. Divide it into 30 equal sized portions. Smooth and shape each portion into an imperfect ball, about 2 and ½ to 3 inches in size. Roll each portion of dough in the bread crumbs and place in the baking sheet.

- Allow little spaces in between portions. Cover the rolls with kitchen towel and let rise for 30 minutes.
- Preheat oven to 350 F. Bake the pandesal for 20 –25 minutes or until the top is lightly golden.
- Serve warm. Store leftovers in a tightly closed container at room temperature.

CHAPTER FOURTEEN

RYE BREAD VARIETIES

Rye, like wheat, has bread making potential and rye dough can develop; however, rye bread does not have the potential for expansion that wheat bread does. It is higher in fiber than white bread and is often darker in color and stronger in flavor.

Rye flour is also high in pentosan gums—about four times as much as wheat flour. The gums give some structure to rye breads, but they also interfere with gluten development and make rye doughs stickier than wheat doughs.

Rye flour is milled much like wheat flour. The lightest rye flours, from the inner part of the kernel, have a low extraction rate, corresponding to patent flour. The following grades and types are generally available –

- **Light rye** – The lightest is nearly white. It has a very fine texture and a high percentage of starch, with little protein.
- **Medium rye** – This is straight flour, milled from the whole rye grain after the bran is removed. Thus, it is darker than light rye and has higher protein content.

- **Dark rye** – Like clear flour milled from wheat, dark rye comes from the part of the rye grain closest to the bran. Thus, it is darker than other rye flours and has a lower percentage of fine starch particles.
- **Whole rye flour** – This product is made from the whole rye kernel, including the bran and germ.
- **Rye meal or pumpernickel flour** – Rye meal is a dark, coarse meal made from the entire ryegrain, including the bran and germ. Products labeled pumpernickel are sometimes cut intoflakes rather than ground into coarse meal. Rye meal is used for pumpernickel bread andsimilar specialty products.
- **Rye blend** – This is a mixture of rye flour (generally 25 to 40%) and strong wheat flour,such as clear flour.

Rye will grow under much harsher conditions than wheat. In Germany and Scandinavia rye breads, either wholly rye or mixed with other grains, are eaten. In the UK, rye is little used and the somewhat bitter flavour that it imparts is in general not appreciated.

The small amount of rye used is deployed in health food products, crisp breads and in making rye products to satisfy foreign tastes.Pure rye bread contains only rye flour, without any wheat, like German –style *Pumpernickel*, a dark, dense, and close – textured loaf, is made from crushed or ground whole rye grains, usually without wheat flour, baked for long periods at a low temperature in a covered tin.

German *Schwarzbrot* or *black bread* and Danish *rugbrød* is made using sour dough starter. The German *Vollkornbrot* (whole –grain bread) contains both rye meal and cracked whole rye grains (which are generally soaked overnight before incorporating into the dough).

There are three different types of rye crispbread– yeast fermented, sourdough fermented and cold bread crispbread. Most of the crispbread produced in Scandinavia is baked following three to four hours of fermentation. Sourdough crispbreads are used in Finland, Estonia, Latvia, Lithuania, Poland, Germany and India. Jewish rye bread refers to a type of rye bread commonly made in Jewish communities and is called *sissel bread* or *cissel bread.*

In Scandinavia, similar bread is made, called *limpa* also include sweeteners and/or citrus peel, as well as spices such as anise, fennel or cardamom, sometimes reserved for festive occasions.

Recipe of Pumpernickel:

Ingredients –

- Warm milk – 2 cups
- Vegetable oil – 2 tbsps
- Molasses – 4 tbsps
- Bread flour – 3 ¼ cups
- Rye flour –1 ⅓ cups
- Cornmeal – ½ cup
- Salt –1 ⅓ tsps
- Active dry yeast – 2 ⅔ tsps
- Unsweetened cocoa powder – 4 tbsps
- Brown sugar –2 ⅔ tbsps

Method –

- Mix well bread flour, rye flour, cornmeal, salt, yeast, cocoa, and brown sugar. Add milk, oil, and molasses.

- Mix thoroughly. When mixed well enough that the dough holds together, knead by hand 15 –20 minutes.
- Cover, let rise in bowl 30 minutes. Punch down, form, and place into 9 1/2x5 inch pan.
- Cover with damp cloth and let rise about 1 hour.
- Bake in preheated 375 degree F (190 degrees C) oven 25 to 30 minutes, covering top with aluminum foil last 10 minutes.

CHAPTER FIFTEEN

CORNMEAL BREAD

Corn is perhaps the most important grain flours and meals after wheat and rye. (In Great Britain, corn is referred to as *maize*, while the word *corn* simply means “grain”). Corn contains no gluten –forming proteins, although it does contain significant quantities of other proteins, and is therefore important in vegetarian diets. Because this ingredient lacks gluten, it does not expand upon baking and often results in dense structure.

Corn is most often used by the baker in the form ofblue, purple, yellow and white cornmeal (depending on the corn color itself). Blue cornmeal is also available. Most cornmeal is made from only the endosperm, because the oil in the germ becomes rancid quickly.

However, whole – grain cornmeal is also available. Cornmeal is available in grinds from fine, medium, and coarse grains. Coarse cornmeal produces a crumbly, somewhat gritty texture in cornbreads, a quality that is desirable in some products. In India it is caked *“Makke ka atta”*.

Cornbreadscan be made in two types– Rich cornbreads made without flour that use eggs to bind the bread and temper the cornmeal and baking soda to raise it and those that have about equal amounts of cornmeal and flour like in corn yeast breads such as muffins, cakes, spoon bread and for lining the bottom of baking pans when baking bread, pizzas, focaccia, etc. Cornbreads tend to be crumbly in texture and do not keep well. .

Recipe of Corn Bread

Ingredients –

- Cornmeal –1 cup (120g)
- All –purpose flour –1 cup (125g)
- Baking powder –1 tsp
- Baking soda – ½ tsp
- Salt –1/8 tsp
- Unsalted butter, melted and slightly cooled – ½cup (115g)
- Light or dark brown sugar –1/3 cup (67g)
- Honey –2 tbsps (30ml)
- Egg, at room temperature –1 large
- Buttermilk, at room temperature –1 cup (240ml)

Method –

- Preheat oven to 400°F (204°C). Grease and lightly flour an 8 or 9 –inch square baking pan. Set aside.
- Whisk the cornmeal, flour, baking powder, baking soda, and salt together in a large bowl. Set aside.
- In a medium bowl, whisk the melted butter, brown sugar, and honey together until completely smooth and thick. Then, whisk in the egg until combined.
- Finally, whisk in the buttermilk. Pour the wet ingredients into the dry ingredients and whisk until combined. Avoid over –mixing.

- Pour batter into prepared baking pan. Bake for 20 minutes or until golden brown on top and the center is cooked through. Use a toothpick to test.
- Edges should be crispy at this point.
- Allow to slightly cool before slicing and serving. Serve cornbread with butter, honey, jam, or whatever you like.
- Wrap leftovers up tightly and store at room temperature for up to 1 week.

Recipe of Corn Muffin

Ingredients –

- Cornmeal – (150 gms or 5 1/3 ounces) 1 cup
- All –purpose flour – (140 gms or 5 ounces) 1 cup
- Sugar, optional – (50 gms or 1 3/4 ounces) ¼ cup
- Baking powder – 1 tbsp
- Salt – 3/4 tsp
- Milk (whole or 2%) – 1 cup
- Vegetable or canola oil – 1/3 cup
- Large eggs –2
-

Method –

- Preheat the oven to 425°F. Spray 12 regular –size muffin cups with butter. Set aside.
- In a large bowl, whisk together the cornmeal, flour, sugar, baking powder and salt.
- In a 2 cup measure, measure the milk, then the oil. Add the eggs and whisk to mix.

- Pour the wet ingredients over the dry ingredients and stir just until it is mostly mixed. Some lumps are fine.
- Fill the cups 7/8 full (almost full). Bake for 12 to 14 minutes until lightly
- Can be stored for 1 –2 days at room temperature and for 1 week in refrigerator.

CHAPTER SIXTEEN

WHOLE WHEAT BREAD

Whole wheat bread or wholemeal bread or whole grain bread or graham flouris a type of bread made using flour that is partly or entirely milled from whole or almost – whole wheat grains, see whole –wheat flour and whole grain. It is called wheat flour to distinguish it from rye flour, corn flour, oat flour, or rice flour. It is one kind of *brown bread*.

The exact composition of products legally marketable as "whole wheat bread" varies from country to country and even within one country. In some cases, the bread is made with whole –grain flour that contains all of the component parts of the grain in the same ratios as they occur in nature, whereas in other cases the bread may include only representative amounts of bran or wheat germ. It is a healthier alternative, because whole wheat flour has a lot more fiber and nutrition than the more processed white flours.

In Canada, for example, a proportion of the wheat germ may be removed from the flour to reduce the risk of rancidity, but the term "whole –wheat bread" is still used. Whole wheat is much higher in fiber, vitamins B6 and E, magnesium, zinc, folic acid and chromium with respect to its partner whole white bread which contains fewer nutrients.

Whole wheat flour does not keep as long as white flour because of the fat contained in the wheat germwhich easily oxidizes to rancid off flavors. Bread made from whole wheat flour is heavier than bread made with white flour, so most of the time, a combination is used.

Whole wheat bread requires a shorter fermentation time due to the enzyme activity in the germ of the wheat grain, and the higher water content in the dough. Whole wheat bread doughs are less cohesive and resilient than those made with bread flour, and 100 percent whole wheat bread is denser and coarser than white bread. It is also darker in color and stronger in flavor.

Recipe

Ingredients –

- Whole wheat flour – 2 ½cups
- Instant dry yeast – 1 tbsp
- Sugar – 2 tbsp
- Salt – 3/4 tsp
- Olive oil – 2 tbsp
- Whole wheat flour – for sprinkling
- Butter – for brushing
-

Method –

- To make whole wheat bread, combine the yeast, sugar and ¼ cup of warm water in a bowl, cover it with a lid and keep aside for 10 minutes.

- Combine the whole wheat flour, salt and yeast –sugar mixture in a deep bowl, mix well and knead into soft dough using enough warm water.
- Add the olive oil and knead very well till the dough is smooth.
- Shape the dough into a proper round using both your hands while tucking the edges at the bottom.
- Cover it with a dry muslin cloth and keep aside in a warm place for 45 minutes or till the dough is double in size.
- Sprinkle the whole wheat flour over a smooth, flat surface, place the dough over it and knead it very well using both your hands. If the dough is getting sticky while kneading, then sprinkle little whole wheat flour as required.
- Tap the dough with your fingers and spread it to make a 250mm. x 200 mm. (10" x 8") diameter oval shape.
- Roll the dough to make a 200 mm. (8") long cylindrical roll and place it in a greased bread loaf tin. Cover it with a dry muslin cloth and again keep aside in a warm place for 30 minutes.
- Bake it in a pre –heated oven at 200°C (400°F) for 10 minutes.
- Lower the temperature to 180°C (360°F) and bake it for 30 minutes.
- Brush the whole wheat bread loaf with butter and keep aside to cool slightly.
- Once the whole wheat bread loaf is slightly cooled, de –mould it and keep aside to cool completely.
- Once the whole wheat bread loaf has cooled completely, cut it into desired slices.
- Serve or use the whole wheat bread as required.

CHAPTER SEVENTEEN

RAISIN BREAD

This is a soft roll variety in which is made with straight dough method with raisins and sometimes flavoured with cinnamon. Apart from white flour, this bread can be made with other flours such as all –purpose flour, oat flour, or whole wheat flour.

It is said that this particular bread was prepared by appeared in Henry David Thoreau in Concord, Massachusetts and the recipe was published in 1671 and was widely appreciated throughout Europe. *Stollen*of Germany is a Christmas cake, *Kulich* was Easter bread made in Russia and *Panettone*was made in Italy.

It has become a popular tea recipe of Europe, particularly England. In the 1920s, raisin bread was advertised as *"The Bread of Iron"*, due to the high iron content of the raisins.

It can be also eaten in many forms, including being served toasted for breakfast *"raisin toast"* or made into sandwiches. Some restaurants serve raisin bread with their cheeseboards

Recipe

Ingredients –

- Active dry yeast – 2 ¼ tsp

- Warm water – ¼ cup
- Raisins – 1 cup
- Butter (softened) – ¼ cup
- Granulated sugar – ¼ cup
- Salt – ½ tsps
- Milk (warm) – ½ cup
- All –purpose flour (divided) 3 ¾ cups
- Large eggs (beaten) – 2

Method –

- Dissolve the yeast in the warm water.
- In a large bowl, combine the raisins, butter, sugar, salt, and warm milk; stir to dissolve the sugar. Let the mixture cool to lukewarm.
- Stir 1 ½ cups of the flour into the milk mixture and beat until smooth.
- Add the yeast mixture and the beaten eggs to the milk mixture and mix to blend well.
- Add enough of the remaining flour to make soft but stiff dough.
- Turn the dough out onto a lightly floured surface and knead for about 10 minutes,
- or until the dough is smooth and elastic.
- Butter or oil a large bowl. Place the dough in the greased bowl. Turn it over to grease the entire surface of the dough.
- Cover the bowl with a clean kitchen towel and let it stand in a warm, draft – free place until it has doubled in bulk, about 1 to 1 ½ hours.
- Punch the dough down and divide it into two equal portions. Cover the dough with a kitchen towel and let it rest for 10 minutes.

- Shape the dough into two loaves and place them in two greased 8 –by –4 – inch loaf pans.
- Cover the pans with a kitchen towel and let the loaves rise for about 45 to 60 minutes, or until the dough has almost doubled in bulk.
- Bake at 3750F for 25 minutes. Place foil over the loaves for the last 10 minutes if they look overly brown.
- Remove the loaves from the pans and let them cool on racks.

CHAPTER EIGHTEEN

CHEESE BREAD

Cheese bread or bun may be referred to variety of small, baked, cheese –flavored rolls, a popular snack and breakfast food in U S A and South America. In countries where the snack is popular, it is inexpensive and often sold from street vendors, in snack shops, and in grocery stores.

The bread was created by accident when CoraliaHarn of Stella's Bakery simply mixed the *Empanada* (Indian gujia type snacks) filling into bread dough.

This bread quickly became an important part of Madison's food culture and quickly spread across the continents.

It was named by the Wisconsin state journal as one of 30 plates that define Madison. Today, the bread is made with brioche –like yeasted dough, mixed with cheese and topped with crushed hot red peppers.It may also contains chives and parsley.

The bread is often eaten as snack bread, pulled apart and eaten while walking around the farmers market.

It is called *Almojábana* –throughout South America, *Chipa* –Paraguay, *Chipá* – Argentina, *Cuñapé* –Bolivia, Pandebono –Colombia, *Pan de queso* –Colombia, *Pan de yuca* –Colombia and Ecuador, *Pão de queijo* –Brazil. The type of cheese varies according to preference or availability. The most used are mozzarella, cheddar and parmesan.

Recipe

Ingredients –

- All –purpose flour – 1 ¾ cups
- White sugar – ¼ cup
- Baking powder – 2 ½ tsps
- Salt – ¾ tsp
- Shredded cheddar cheese – 1 cup
- Garlic powder – ½ tsp
- Minced herbs – ¼ cup (parsley and chives)
- Egg – 1 beaten
- Milk – ¾ cup
- Vegetable oil – ⅓ cup

Method –

- Preheat oven to 400⁰F (200⁰C). Lightly grease a 9x5 inch loaf pan.
- In a large bowl, mix together flour, sugar, baking powder, salt and cheese. In another large bowl, beat together egg, milk and oil.
- Stir the flour/cheese mixture/ garlic/minced herb into the egg mixture, stirring until just moistened.
- Pour batter into prepared pan.
- Bake in preheated oven for 35 minutes, until a toothpick inserted into center of loaf comes out clean.

CHAPTER NINETEEN

INDIGENOUS BREADS OF INDIA

Indian breads have found place in history since the Vedic period, thousands of years back. There are mentions of popular "Paratha" which loosely translates to stuffed bread offered to the Devas (Indian Gods) during religious rituals. One of the most famous Hindu epics written by Tulsidas in the 16th century the Ramayana, mentions the word "Roti" in quite a few verses. Even the literature of South India has mentions various types of breads in their various texts. For Indian no meal is complete until these are served along with and in some parts it is the staple food of the people.

When it comes to bread, we immediately tend to imagine French or Italian bakeries or English bakeries with hot loaves baking in the oven. All Indians have accepted these breads as an intrinsic part of our culture albeit in different forms and in their daily food habits.

Indians relish on its own brand of different types of indigenous breads called in different dailects as chapati, roti, phulka, paratha, naan, Kulcha, poori, luchi, appam, bati, bakshalu, adai, bhatoora etc.

Roti – is a flatbread made from wholemeal flour, traditionally known as atta. It is also called *Chapati* or

Phulka. The beauty of roti's is that they can be eaten with anything.*Thalipeeth* is multi –grain bread flat bread made from roasted tapioca, Rajgira, coriander seeds, cumin seeds, wheat, and rice. *Tandoori roti* is prepared in tandoor. *Joladarotti* is an unleavened Indian bread made out of jowar, originating from state of North Karnataka. It is coarser than a roti and can be either soft or hard in texture. *Sheermal* is a saffron – flavored traditional flatbread made in India. It is one of the special preparations of the cities of Lucknow and Hyderabad in India.*Pathiri* is a soft chapati like bread made of rice flour. It is part of the local cuisine of coastal Malabar region in Southern India.*Roomali roti* is a thin flatbread originating from the Indian subcontinent, popular in India and in Punjab and Delhi. It is eaten with tandoori dishes.

Paratha – Paratha is a flat, thick piece of unleavened bread fried on a griddle. Parathas come in two primary forms– plain or stuffed. They are famous in North India and served with butter, pickle and yogurt. Tandoori paratha is prepared in tandoor which has spiral flakes (Lachchha paratha). Bhakri – Hard and crisp, it is unleavened bread made with flour and is popular in Maharashtra, Goa and Gujarat.*Thepla* is a flatbread similar to paratha, made of whole wheat flour, oil and spice powders like turmeric, red chili powder etc.It is soft and has a longer shelf life than most bread.

Luchi or poori – flat deep fried bread made of either whole wheatflour or refined wheat flour (maida). This is widely eaten and can be eaten with any kind of dal or vegetable.*Kachori*is thicker than poori and is stuffed with a variety of ingredients like peas, onion, potato, mawa etc. Its close cousin is Bengali *Radhabalabhi* which is also a type of stuffed poori, but is thinner than kachori.*Bhatura* is Deep fried crispy leavened bread much larger in size than poori served with Chhole. Bedmi – urad dal stuffed poori generally eaten with potato curry in breakfast in Northern India.

Baati – Baati is hard, unleavened bread cooked in state of Rajasthan, and in some parts of state of Madhya Pradesh and Gujarat. Baati is always eaten with dal. Similar to this is *Litti*, which is stuffed with *Sattu* (roasted chana and roasted jowar ground together) and cooked in live charcoal and eaten with *chokha* (spiced mashed brinjal)

Puran Poli – It is stuffed pan fried flat bread with a sweet filling made from skinned split bengal gram /chana dal and jaggery. Sweet filling is puran and bread is called as poli. Similarly *Makuni* is flat bread stuffed with Sattu and pan fried.*Bakshalu* is moong dal stuffed sweet Indian flat bread from Telengana. *Thepla* are flatbreads made from fresh fenugreek leaves, whole wheat flour and gram flour (besan).

Taftan – is leavened flour bread from Iranian origin and popular Mughlai bread made with eggs, flour, saffron, spices and kneaded in milk. *Bakarkhani* is a leavened bread and has a biscuit like texture. It is mildly spiced, is sweet and is flavoured with saffron.*Naan* – oven –baked elongated shaped leavened flat bread made from maida. *Girda or khameer*is soft leavened bread from Kashmir.

CHAPTER TWENTY

BAKERY BREADS OF INDIA

White Breads: It is the most popular and common bread with 400g or 800g packs.White bread is made up from wheat flour minus the bran and the germ. White breads are the later fortified with minerals and vitamins. These breads are sold as whole uncut packs or sliced into pieces.

Whole wheat grain bread or Brown Bread: Whole wheat bread contains the bran and germ which are not segregated as in white bread hence it has got better nutritional value.It is brownish colour because it contains the outer pericarp and aleurone layers of the wheat grain.

Sandwich bread: It is white bread with larger dimensions .These meant for the commercial use of sandwiches for hotels, restaurants and offices.School children also prefer these types of breads.

Flavoured Breads: Bread Manufacturers with a view to local taste add flavours, spices to match the palate, creating varieties such as daliya,basil, garlic, onion, or cinnamon.

Paav: Indian equivalents to burger buns.Pav or pao are basically a small loaf of bread, introduced by the Portuguese in India. These are very popular in city of Mumbai (vada pav) and pavbhaji. These are breads made with whole –wheat flour instead of refined wheat flour. They are brown in colour outside as well as inside, but as fluffy as the white bread.*Bombay bundt bread* is the specialty of Mumbai. This bread is flower in shape prepared in Bundt pan. The center of this bread is filled with bhaji (curry) and served.

Exotic Breads: Retail bakery chains are promoting exotic breads with chefs brought from Europe or Latin America.Baguettes, rolls, paninis, ciabattas, multi –grain bread, croissants, foccaccias, organic breads and gluten–free breads.

Fruity Bread: Some bread manufacturers attract kids with their own style of breads filled with tutti fruity bits, chocolate chips and soft candies.

Recipe of Bombay Bun bread

Ingredients –

- Refined flour – 2 cups
- Salt – 1 tsp
- Sugar – 1 tbsp
- Warm milk – 3/4 cup
- Fresh cream – ¼ cup
- Milk powder – 7 tbsps
- Canola oil – 2 tbsp
- Yeast mixture
- Yeast – 2 tbsps
- Warm water – 1 tbsp
- Sugar – 1 tsp
- Milk and butter mixture for the golden crust
- Milk – 1 tbsp
- Salted butter – 2 tbsps

Method –

- Firstly, in a small bowl, put the yeast with one tbsp warm water and one tsp sugar. Let rest for 5 mins (yeast mixture).
- In a big bowl, put the flour, salt, sugar, and milk powder. Mix well.
- Make a well in the center of the dry ingredients. Add the warm milk, fresh cream, one tbsp of canola oil and the yeast mixture. Mix well.
- Bring the mixture onto a flat surface and knead well for 5 –7 minutes.
- Add the remaining tbsp of oil and knead well (3 –4 mins) until the dough is soft and smooth.
- Cling wrap the dough and keep in a warm place for about an hour. The dough should double in size.
- Punch the dough and knead for about a minute. Form round balls and place in a greased bundt pan. Make sure the pan is well greased with butter or oil.
- Keep this in a warm place and let it rise again.
- Once double in size make a mixture of butter and warm milk and apply onto the dough using a brush. This gives the bread a golden brown crust.
- Cover the bundt baking dish with foil and bake in a preheated oven at 400^0F (200^0C) for 25 to 30 minutes.
- Once baked, brush on some butter and serve.

Recipe of Fruit Bread

Ingredients –
For The yeast batter:

- Strong white bread flour – 100 gms
- Yeast – 5 gms
- Sugar – 1tsp
- Lukewarm milk – 250ml

For the dough:

- Strong white bread flour – 350 gms
- Unsalted butter – 50 gms
- Sugar – 50 gms
- Salt – ½tsp
- Cashew nuts – 25 gms
- Pistachio – 25 gms
- Almonds – 25 gms
- Walnuts – 25 gms
- Raisins – 25 gms
- Sultanas – 25 gms
- Sweetened dried apple/cranberries – 25 gms
- Chopped dates – 25 gms
- Cinnamon powder – ½tsp
- Egg – 1 no
-

Method –

- Chop all nuts and dried fruits (except raisins and sultanas) into same size bits.
- Mix together flour, yeast and sugar under the yeast batter. Now slowly beat in the milk to make a smooth batter.
- Cover with foil and leave for about 20 minutes until frothy.

- In a separate large bowl, mix in flour and salt. Rub in the butter.
- Mix in cinnamon powder, sugar and fruits. Beat the eggs. Mix it to the yeast batter. Mix in the flour and fruit mixture. Use a spatula to mix in the dough thoroughly.
- Knead the dough, add if necessary little flour, until it is smooth and no longer sticky.
- Cover with foil and leave it in the bowl, in a warm place for about 50 –60 minutes, until risen and doubled in quantity.
- Butter a 900 gram loaf tin. Spread the dough evenly. Do not press down. Only fill till three –quarters, as it will rise.
- Set the oven temperature to 200^{0}C/400^{0}F/Gas Mark 6. Bake in the centre of the oven for 20 minutes.
- Now loosely cover with foil sheet and bake for another 25 minutes. To check if loaf is cooked, take a skewer, pierce it through the middle, and if it comes out dry then it is done.
- If the skewer returns with moist dough, then it needs at least 10 –15 minutes more.
- Remove from the oven. Allow to cool completely. Slice and serve.
- Serve with tea or coffee.

Recipe of Multi –grain Bread

Ingredients –

- Wheat flour–2cups
- Ragi (nachni / red millet) flour –¼ cup
- Jowar (white millet) flour –¼ cup

- Bajra (black millet) flour –¼ cup
- Powdered flaxseeds (alsi) –1 tbsp
- Sesame seeds (til) –1 tsp
- Melon seeds (charmagaz) –1 tsp
- Quick cooking rolled oats –1 tsp
- Gluten powder – ¼ tsp
- Calcium propionate powder – a pinch
- Salt –1 tsp
- Instant dry yeast –1 tbsp
- Castor sugar –1 tbsp
- Wholeragi (nachni / red millet) – ½tsp
- Bajra (black millet)– ½tsp
- Quick cooking rolled oats –1 tsp
- Flax seeds – ½tsp

Method –

- To make multigrain bread, combine the yeast, sugar and ¼ cup of warm water in a bowl and mix well. Cover it with a lid and keep aside for 10 minutes.
- Combine all the remaining ingredients along with the yeast –sugar mixture in a deep bowl, mix well and knead into loose sticky dough using approx. 1 ½ cups of warm water.
- Place the dough in a greased bread loaf tin of 200 mm. (8”). Wet your fingers and press the dough lightly to spread it evenly.
- Sprinkle the prepared topping evenly over it, cover it with a dry muslin cloth and keep aside in a warm place for 30 minutes.
- Bake it in a pre –heated oven at 210°C (420°F) for 20 minutes.

- Lower the temperature to 160°C (320°F) and bake it for 10 minutes. Keep aside to cool slightly.
- Once the bread loaf has cooled slightly, de –mould it and cut it into 13 mm. (½”) bread slices.
- Serve the multigrain bread or use as required.

CHAPTER TWENTY-ONE

MIDDLE EASTERN PITA BREAD

Pita or pitta, is most widely consumed bread belonging to a family of yeast –leavened round flatbreads baked from wheat flour, common in the Mediterranean, Middle East, and neighboring areas. This is referred to inArabic simply as *khubz*, meaning "bread".

It is a soft, moist and light bread that is made from all –purpose flour, whole wheat flour, sugar, warm milk, salt with or without instant yeast. This bread with very little leavening that puffs up spectacularly like an odd –looking balloon after a few minutes in a hot oven over stone or skillet or griddle on stove.

It is a one of the prehistoric flatbreads of the Middle East with evidence from about 14,500 years ago, during the Stone Age in Jordan.

Today it isserved with meals whole, or cut or broken into wedges for dipping into local sauces or dips, such as *babaghanoush* or *hummus*. Sometimes the pocket breads are stuffed with meats, *falafel* topped with *tahini* sauce, or as wrap for *kebabs* and *gyros*with ingredients to create a sandwich.

It can also be cut and baked into crispy pita chips.Traditional pitta bread is made by a sour dough process but it can bemade using manufactured yeast. If the sour dough process is used, arelatively large portion of sour dough (approximately 20%) is used, giving a more rapid fermentation than most sour dough products.

Recipe

Ingredients –

For sour dough

- Fresh compressed yeast –15 gms or 2tbsp
- Granulated sugar –1 tbsp
- Luke warm water –1 ½ cups (360 ml)
- Bread flour –400 gms

For dough

- Luke warm water –1 ½ cups (360 ml)
- Salt –20 gms or 4 tsp
- Olive oil - 80 ml
- Bread flour –570 gms

Method –

- To make the sponge, dissolve the yeast and sugar in the warm water, then add the bread flour.
- Mix until well blended and smooth, then cover and let stand in a warm place until the sponge has doubled in bulk, approximately 30 minutes.
- To make the dough, add the warm water to the sponge together with the salt, olive oil, and all but a handful of the bread flour.

- Knead, using the dough hook on low speed, until the dough forms a smooth and elastic ball, about 8 minutes.
- Place the dough on a worktable and knead in as much of the reserved flour by hand as needed to prevent the dough from being sticky.
- Work the dough into a firm ball and place in a lightly oiled bowl. Turn to coat with oil, then cover and let proof in a warm place for 1 ½ hours.
- Punch down the dough and divide into 16 equal pieces about 4 ounces (115 g) each.
- Shape the pieces into tight round balls.
- Cover and set aside on a floured surface for 30 minutes to let the dough proof and the gluten relax.
- Before starting to form the breads, preheat the oven to 475°F (246°C).
- Flatten and roll out each ball of dough to a 7 –inch (17.5 –cm) disk, using flour to prevent it from sticking.
- There should not be any wrinkles or cuts in the dough that can prevent the pitas from forming pockets as they bake.
- Lay the dough rounds on floured towels or baking pans after rolling them.
- Let stand at room temperature until they have puffed slightly.
- Starting with the breads rolled out first, use a floured peel to slide 4 pitas at a time directly onto the hearth of the oven.
- Bake for approximately 4 minutes or until light golden brown on the bottom.
- The breads should puff up halfway through baking.
- If the breads become too dark on the bottom before they are firm on the top, lower the heat slightly.
- Place on wire racks to cool.

- Cover it with a dry towel if you would like to keep the crust soft.
- Bake the remaining pita breads in the same way.
- Once the breads have cooled, if they are not to be served right away, wrap them in plastic to keep them flexible.
- Freeze for longer storage.

CHAPTER TWENTY-TWO

FRENCH AND ITALIAN BREADS AND ROLLS

Italy and France specialize in the making of bread, but one will find it difficult to find any differences between the two. Anything from the bread's baking method down to its shape and size is usually done in a different way on either side of the French –Italian border. Some of the most common variations to look out for include the differences in bread dough and the ingredients used.

The common difference between the breads and rolls of these countries are –

Both Italy and France are countries that specialize in bread making. Sure, when we sit down to eat at a restaurant in the US we are given a bread basket to start off our dinner. But bread is essential to almost every meal in Italy and France.

If the bread supply ran out in either of these countries, you can expect riots in the streets. However, the two countries approach bread-making quite differently from one another.

Baguettes, focaccia, brioche— all of these bread differ vastly in size, shape, and how they are served. Regardless of differences, as Americans, we enjoy these breads on a daily basis.

If you want to know a little more about how these breads are created in their native countries and what sets them apart, take a look at what I have come up with below.

When we think of French bread, the "French stick" usually comes to mind. It is a long, thin crusty loaf that is typically referred to as a "baguette," which directly translates into "a stick."

The Baguette may be the most popular type of bread in France—it is eaten throughout almost every province in the country—but it is certainly not the only kind made.

Other types of ordinary French white bread include the couronne, which is bread in the shape of a ring, or "country bread" (pain de Campagne) which often incorporates whole wheat or rye flour in its ingredients.

In terms of Italian bread making, the paesanos are known to allow the yeast to fully rise over the course of a few hours, resulting in a very thin-crusted loaf. The interior of Italian bread is typically extremely moist and absorbent—the better to soak up olive oil and tomatoes from Caprese.

Types of Italian bread include ciabatta— made of wheat flour and yeast—piadina, made of flour, lard, and salt—and panettone, a bread that is native to Milan. Both countries make delicious loaves, but the similarities between Italian and French bread end the moment you compare the two side by side.

The first way to distinguish Italian from French bread is to simply eyeball the two. French and Italian bread comes in all shapes and sizes. However, to broadly generalize, while French bread is long with rounded edges, Italian bread comes in a more overall circular shape.

French bread is typically baked in a long, thin shape and has become the major food symbol of the country. The baguette can be baked as long as 30 inches and is a staple in almost every region.

On the other hand, Italian bread is known to be baked in more a flat and round shape. Italian loaves are also shorter and typically thicker than their French counterparts. Although it is possible to get baguette-type-looking bread in an Italian bakery, on average, most Italian bread is shaped into larger rounds.

There are endless variations in the size and shape of bread in each country, but these are the major indicators that will distinguish the two.

Because bread comes with every French and Italian meal, you might think they are served for the same reasons. However, In France, bread is usually given as a starter. French brioche, a sweet bread, is even eaten in the morning with breakfast meals. The French also employ the baguette as a multipurpose bread, used for sandwiches and as the base for canapés

Italian bread, on the other hand, is usually served as a supplement to pasta or other main courses. A side dish, if you will. Italians eat bread to absorb the flavors of olive oils or the thick sauces in a rich meal.

Although there are vast differences, classic French and Italian bread are, for the most part, made with the same ingredients in a similar fashion. However, one major difference in ingredients is that bread making in France is more tightly controlled than in Italy.

By law in France, bread cannot have added oil or fat. French baguettes, for instance, must be made from water, flour, yeast, and salt, with a very little amount of dough improver allowed.

Italian bread often contains a little bit more milk, olive oil, and sometimes sugar in its contents. Thus, Italians seem to be working with wetter dough as their base than the French.

Like their pizzas, Italian bread is often baked in a flat stone oven. Pane di Genzano, for instance, is a fragrant bread from Lazio, a region located in the central peninsular section of the country, that is usually cooked in a wood fire or stone oven. This particular style of baking gives the bread a signature smoky flavor and pungent aroma.

Conversely, the French are known for using electric convection deck ovens. This method of baking gives the loaf an overall softer texture. They bake their bread usually at the same temperatures as the Italians.

France is famous for its brioche, a sweet bread that is made with unsalted butter and eggs that are added to the dough to give it a"sugary sweet" taste. There are all types of bread in France, but typically, they make sweeter loaves than the Italians—just think of French toast!

Italy is famed for its savory bread. One, in particular, is focaccia, a flat oven-baked product that is similar to pizza dough in texture. Typically focaccia is topped with herbs and other savory ingredients such as olive oil or salt. Another exquisite savory Italian bread is Pane Casareccio, a popular rustic stuffed bread.

While the French usually stick to the sweets, Italians embrace the savories.

Not all French bread falls under the category of baguette. Take a look.

Baguettes are long, thin loaves of white bread made from a basic dough. Incisions are cut into the top of the loaf to allow it to expand and give the bread its trademark appearance. As stated earlier, the dough for baguettes is defined by French law, and only small variations are allowed in terms of ingredients.

Two types of baguettes are generally available in France: traditional and commercial. The traditional baguette is made of only wheat flour, water, salt, and yeast.

Commercial baguettes are sold in supermarkets and often found in restaurants. In addition to the main ingredients used in traditional baguettes, commercial baguettes also contain additives. The yeast typically used in commercial baguettes is "levure" instead of "levain."

Levure yeast allows the bread to rise much faster for commercial purposes. Without additives, baguettes do not keep well because they contain no fat.

In the U.S., the term "French bread" refers to a loaf of a certain shape, i.e., a long and thin stick. But outside the United States, “French bread” can refer to all different types of the loaf, including, but not limited to the standard baguette.

Other types of French bread include ficelle (a small, thin baguette), or pain de Campagne which is a rounded loaf containing sourdough. Each region in France has its own specialty bread, some of the most notable being fig and walnut which is characteristic of the south, and milk bread in the northern region.

CHAPTER TWENTY-THREE

GLOSSARY

- **Aroma**– when bread is smelled, close to the nose, while inhaling deeply, the aromatic sensation experienced is described as bread aroma.
- **Baati** – Baati is hard, unleavened bread cooked in state of Rajasthan, and in some parts of state of Madhya Pradesh and Gujarat. Baati is always eaten with dal. Similar to this is Litti, which is stuffed with Sattu (roasted chana and roasted jowar ground together) and cooked in live charcoal and eaten with chokha (spiced mashed brinjal)
- **Break and shred**– break and shred should be high and fairly smooth, not excessive or rough or bulging.
- **Brioche** –is classic French yeast very 'rich' bread. Whereas standard breads can be made only with water, flour, salt and yeast, a brioche will contain plenty eggs, milk and butter. The high fat and protein contents of these ingredients are what make the bread so special. Fresh brioche can be served with jelly or other preserves to accompany tea or coffee, or with pate or hors d'oeuvre.
- **Buns** – is a small, sometimes sweet, bread based item or roll. Though they come in many shapes and sizes,

they are most commonly hand –sized or smaller, with a round top and flat bottom. They are usually made from flour, sugar, milk, yeast and butter. Common sweet varieties contain small fruit or nuts, and may topped with icing or caramel, or filled with jam or cream. Some types of buns are filled with various meats, or used to serve meats (such as hotdogs or hamburgers). They are served in every dinner in Great Britain.

- **Challah** –these are braided buns with 3 –6 braids. It is a Jewish specialty. Challah has a noticeably higher level of eggs than the other doughs on this list, which contributes to its especially golden crust and often yellowish interior crumb.
- **Cinnamon Rolls** –are made up of flattened rich dough that has been spread with cinnamon and sugar, then rolled and sliced into glorious swirls of buttery pastry and gooey filling. They are served commonly in Northern Europe and North America. In Sweden it is called kanelbulle, in Denmark it is known as kanelsnegl, in Norway it is known as Skillings boller, It is commonly eaten in breakfast or coffee break or as dessert.
- **Croissant** –or crescent rolls are French buttery, flaky, Viennoiserie pastry of Austrian origin, named for its historical crescent shape. The yeast leavened dough is layered with butter, rolled and folded several times in succession, then rolled into a sheet, in a technique called laminating. The process results in a layered, flaky texture, similar to a puff pastry. They are a common part of a continental breakfast in many European countries.
- **Crumb color**– bright white or slightly creamy.
- **Crust color**– well –developed golden –brown color, smooth and even.

- **Crust surface**– side walls and top crust should be smooth and should not contain holes or pits.
- **Dark rye** – Like clear flour milled from wheat, dark rye comes from the part of the rye grain closest to the bran. Thus, it is darker than other rye flours and has a lower percentage of fine starch particles.
- **Exotic Breads:** Retail bakery chains are promoting exotic breads with chefs brought from Europe or Latin America. Baguettes, rolls, paninis, ciabattas, multi –grain bread, croissants, foccaccias, organic breads and gluten–free breads.
- **Flavor**– slightly sweet, yeasty and aromatic flavor of baker's yeast mixed in flour –and – water dough. Strong and sharp fermentation flavors are not desired.
- **Flavored Breads:** Bread Manufacturers with a view to local taste add flavours, spices to match the palate, creating varieties such as daliya, basil, garlic, onion, or cinnamon.
- **Fruity Bread:** Some bread manufacturers attract kids with their own style of breads filled with tutti fruity bits, chocolate chips and soft candies.
- **Grain**– small (tight) cells, very thin cell walls, fine and uniform cell size distribution in center, elongated and fine cells around perimeter.
- **Light rye** – The lightest is nearly white. It has a very fine texture and a high percentage of starch, with little protein.
- **Loaf volume**– good loaf volume with optimum oven spring. Sufficient rise renders proper break and shred.
- **Luchi or poori** – flat deep fried bread made of either whole wheat flour or refined wheat flour (maida). This is widely eaten and can be eaten with any kind of dal or vegetable. Kachoriis thicker than poori and is stuffed

with a variety of ingredients like peas, onion, potato, mawa etc. Its close cousin is Bengali Radhabalabhi which is also a type of stuffed poori, but is thinner than kachori. Bhatura is Deep fried crispy leavened bread much larger in size than poori served with Chhole. Bedmi – urad dal stuffed poori generally eaten with potato curry in breakfast in Northern India.

- **Medium rye** – This is straight flour, milled from the whole rye grain after the bran is removed. Thus, it is darker than light rye and has higher protein content.
- **Monkey Bread** –The origin of the term "monkey bread" comes from the pastry being a finger food; the consumer would pick apart the bread as a monkey would. This American bread recipe is made in a bundt cake pan to create a donut –shaped cake that's easy to pull apart. It is covered with butter and sugar and sometimes with vanilla ice cream. It can be taken as breakfast, brunch, or dessert.
- **Mouth feel**– moist and soft (dry or gummy mouth feel are not desired).
- **Paav:** Indian equivalents to burger buns. Pav or pao are basically a small loaf of bread, introduced by the Portuguese in India. These are very popular in city of Mumbai (vada pav) and pavbhaji. These are breads made with whole –wheat flour instead of refined wheat flour. They are brown in colour outside as well as inside, but as fluffy as the white bread. Bombay bundt bread is the specialty of Mumbai. This bread is flower in shape prepared in Bundt pan. The center of this bread is filled with bhaji (curry) and served.
- **Paratha** – Paratha is a flat, thick piece of unleavened bread fried on a griddle. Parathas come in two primary forms– plain or stuffed. They are famous in North India

and served with butter, pickle and yogurt. Tandoori paratha is prepared in tandoor which has spiral flakes (Lachchha paratha). Bhakri – Hard and crisp, it is unleavened bread made with flour and is popular in Maharashtra, Goa and Gujarat. Thepla is a flatbread similar to paratha, made of whole wheat flour, oil and spice powders like turmeric, red chili powder etc. It is soft and has a longer shelf life than most bread.

- **Puran Poli** – It is stuffed pan fried flat bread with a sweet filling made from skinned split bengal gram /chana dal and jaggery. Sweet filling is puran and bread is called as poli. Similarly Makuni is flat bread stuffed with Sattu and pan fried. Bakshalu is moong dal stuffed sweet Indian flat bread from Telengana. Thepla are flatbreads made from fresh fenugreek leaves, whole wheat flour and gram flour (besan).
- **Roti** – is a flatbread made from wholemeal flour, traditionally known as atta. It is also called Chapati or Phulka. The beauty of roti's is that they can be eaten with anything. Thalipeeth is multi –grain bread flat bread made from roasted tapioca, Rajgira, coriander seeds, cumin seeds, wheat, and rice. Tandoori roti is prepared in tandoor. Joladarotti is an unleavened Indian bread made out of jowar, originating from state of North Karnataka. It is coarser than a roti and can be either soft or hard in texture. Sheermal is a saffron – flavored traditional flatbread made in India. It is one of the special preparations of the cities of Lucknow and Hyderabad in India.Pathiri is a soft chapati like bread made of rice flour. • It is part of the local cuisine of coastal Malabar region in Southern India. Roomali roti is a thin flatbread originating from the Indian subcontinent, popular in India and in Punjab and Delhi.

It is eaten with tandoori dishes.

- **Sandwich bread:** It is white bread with larger dimensions .These meant for the commercial use of sandwiches for hotels, restaurants and offices. School children also prefer these types of breads.
- **Sticky Buns** –These are a type of dessert or breakfast sweet roll that generally consist of rolled pieces of leavened dough — sometimes containing brown sugar or cinnamon — compressed together to form a kind of flat loaf corresponding to the size of the pan in which they are to be baked. Before the dough is placed in the baking –pan, the latter is lined with the "sticky" ingredients, such as brown sugar, honey (or both), as well as nuts and raisins and perhaps more sugar and sometimes butter. After the buns are baked, they are inverted so that the pan lining then becomes a topping. They originated in Pennsylvania with German settlers.
- **Tactile crumb texture**– smooth and silky feel. Crumb should be resilient when pressing lightly with the fingers.
- **Taftan** – is leavened flour bread from Iranian origin and popular Mughlai bread made with eggs, flour, saffron, spices and kneaded in milk. Bakarkhani is a leavened bread and has a biscuit like texture. It is mildly spiced, is sweet and is flavored with saffron. Naan – oven–baked elongated shaped leavened flat bread made from maida.Girda or khameeriis soft leavened bread from Kashmir.
- **Uniformity of shape**– symmetrical with a rounded top (flat top and irregular shapes are not desired). Loaf should retain a straight and upright position. Keyholing, collapsing, flat top and uneven shape are considered defects.

- **White Breads:** It is the most popular and common bread with 400g or 800g packs.White bread is made up from wheat flour minus the bran and the germ. White breads are the later fortified with minerals and vitamins. These breads are sold as whole uncut packs or sliced into pieces.
- **Whole rye flour** – This product is made from the whole rye kernel, including the bran and germ.
- **Whole wheat grain bread or Brown Bread:** Whole wheat bread contains the bran and germ which are not segregated as in white bread hence it has got better nutritional value. It is brownish color because it contains the outer pericarp and aleurone layers of the wheat grain.

The Author

Dr. Anshumali Pandey is a renowned & reliable name in the field of Education, Hospitality, Tourism and Tribal Food. He is a Teacher and Chef by profession, and also an Author, a Business Auditor, and an avid culinary traveller to the Indian Sub continental hinterlands. Dr. Anshumali Pandey is a Hospitality Educator (PhD) who specialises in Higher Education, Office Administration, Pay roll, HR, Labour Laws, Audit, and Procurement & Tender Process. He is an Author with 76 Publications consisting of 58 Books and 3 short stories.

His contribution and research in the field of Tribal Food, Tribal Tourism, Forest Tourism and Village Tourism in the form of research papers have brought several laurels to him. In 2018 the Ministry of Tourism, Govt of Indian duly recognised all this and awarded him with a National Appreciation certificate and memento.

The books written by **Dr Anshumali Pandey** are essentially a banquet arising from an experience of over 26 years of Professional life and have boiled down to crisp and accurate writing on his favourite subjects. Hospitality Sector champion requires to be a specialist in many fields and Dr Pandey is one of them. His knowledge is evident from the spectrum of subjects which he has chosen for his books so far, which ranges from being a specialist chef, to Master of Human resources, to Education and to love for children, and topped with Spirituality. For more than two decades Dr Pandey has lived with his family in Western India in general and the Tribal belt of the union territory of Dadra & Nagar Haveli in particular. Most of his time is consumed in helping and understanding the Tribal and rural population of the region and writing scholarly articles and books on his vast area of interest.

Books written by the Author are –

1. Theory of Indian Cookery
2. Beauty and Irony of Silvassa Tourism
3. A Short Indian Food Story
4. Be Your Own Guide to Indian Cuisine
5. Cookery Fundamentals
6. History of Indian Food (2 Editions Printed)
7. The Great Indian Story Book for Children
8. Personal Budget: Easy Work Book
9. Online Classes Log Book
10. Dictionary Making Work Book for School Children
11. The Lazy Bed
12. Hindu Dharm (हनि्द्ूधर्म) (In Hindi Language)
13. Where is my coffee?
14. Your First Job is Never your Last (Volume 1)

15. You are Almost There (Quick Fix Resume and Interview Hacks)
16. Working for the Enemy? - A lesson in Career Management
17. Public Speaking for the Young
18. A Date With Coffee
19. How to be The Best Hotel Front Office Employee
20. Diploma in Food Production, The complete Syllabus
21. Diploma in F&B Service, The Complete Syllabus
22. Diploma in Front Office, The Complete Syllabus
23. The Time to Speak is Now
24. Munshi Premchand (Short Stories in English)
25. The Housekeeping Department, Text Book
26. Hitchhiker's Guide to Trekking in Uttarakhand
27. Uttarakhand, A divine Land for a Reason
28. Bachhon ke liye rochak kahaniyan (बच्चों के लिए रोचक कहानियाँ) (In Hindi Language)
29. Basic Communication Skills of English
30. The Basic Office Organisation Book for Start-ups
31. Hospitality HRM
32. Hospitality Marketing
33. Bakery Ingredients and Tools
34. Human Resource Management for Indian Professionals
35. The process of LAWFULLY operating a Hospitality business in India
36. Indian Classical Sweets: History, Tradition and Recipes
37. History of India's Himalayan Cuisine: Classical Cookery of Kashmir, Laddakh, Jammu, Himachal, Lahaul, Spiti, Garhwal, Kumaon.
38. Vindu: Andhra Cuisine (Part 1 of South Indian Trilogy)
39. Saappadu: Tamil Cuisine (Part 2 of South Indian Trilogy)

40. Sadya: Malayali Cuisine (Part 3 of South Indian Trilogy)
41. South Indian Cuisine - The Researcher's Guide Book
42. The Ramayana for Children and other short stories from Indian Mythology
43. Legends of the Tribal Shiva
44. Third Generation Children's Story Book
45. It's Elementary: The Top Nine Adventures from the memoirs of Dr John H Watson
46. UNITY IN DIVERSITY, The foundation of Indian Tourism
47. The Thar Express: Culinary History of Rajasthan and Gujarat
48. Basics of Computerized Accounting
49. Impact (Impact of Globalization on Indian Social Life)
50. Vishnu – The Lord of Amazing Incarnations
51. Being a Mahatma in the Freedom Struggle
52. The Culinary Journey of Purvanchal: Lucknow to Patna
53. Culinary History of the Gangetic Plains
54. Indian Culinary Secrets
55. The Story of Jain and Parsi Food
56. The Great Indian Pilgrimage Tourism
57. Introduction to Tourism Studies – Text Book
58. Bread and Rolls

Connect with me: anshumali.pandey@gmail.com
https://notionpress.com/author/337004

Please scan this QR code on your phone to know more about the latest and complete works of Dr Anshumali Pandey

9 798889 517238

Printed by Libri Plureos GmbH in Hamburg,
Germany